How to Knit

Your Hands-On Guide to Creating Textiles, A Step-by-Step Tutorial

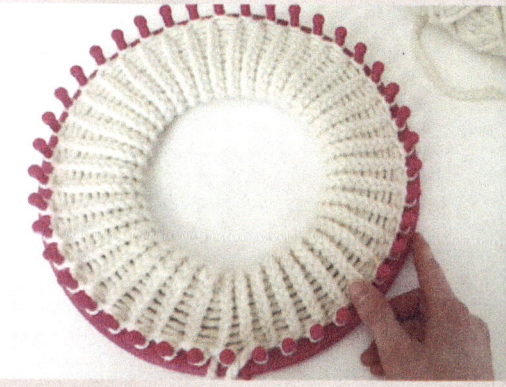

Table of contents

Introduction

We'll begin with the fundamentals, ensuring a solid foundation for your knitting journey. Learn how to choose the right loom, understand the different types of yarn, and master essential techniques like casting on, knitting, purling, and binding off. Each step is explained clearly and concisely, often accompanied by helpful illustrations to guide you visually.

Throughout the book, you'll find a collection of inspiring projects to ignite your creativity. From cozy scarves and warm hats to playful toys and decorative home accessories, these projects cater to all skill levels. Each pattern includes detailed instructions, clear diagrams, and helpful tips to ensure your success.

Whether you're a complete beginner eager to learn a new craft or an experienced knitter seeking a fresh perspective, "How to Loom Knit" will empower you to create beautiful, handmade items with confidence and joy. Let's embark on this knitting adventure together!

SO, WHAT EXACTLY IS LOOM KNITTING?

Rather than two knitting needles like traditional knitting, loom knits are made on a series of pegs. Traditional knitting needles, can be a bit daunting for new crafters, loom knitting pegs act as a framework for your project. This makes it easier to create all sorts of projects like scarves, hats, blankets, and even socks without accidentally dropping stitches!

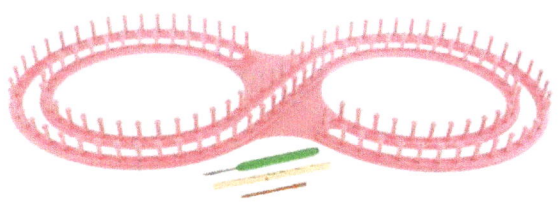

WHY TRY LOOM KNITTING?

One of the biggest advantages of loom knitting is its user-friendly nature. It's incredibly beginner-friendly and doesn't require any prior knitting experience. Crafters of all ages can quickly grasp the basics and start knitting beautiful projects in one session.

The rhythmic motion of working with the loom can also be therapeutic! The action of looping and hooking the yarn on each peg can help you unwind while you create something special with your own hands.

HOW TO LOOM KNIT

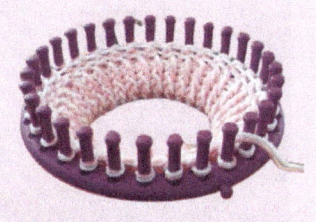

Let's explore now !

ARE KNITTING LOOMS BEGINNER-FRIENDLY?

YES! The knitting loom makes it easy to explore the endless combinations of colors, textures, and yarn types without the stress of dropped stitches.

Don't worry about making mistakes; they are an important part of the learning process. Every project you finish helps you learn a little more and boosts your confidence. We're excited to show you the basics and inspire you to experiment with more intricate designs and techniques as you get to know your knitting loom!

WHAT CAN YOU KNIT WITH A KNITTING LOOM?

You might be surprised how many projects you can make with a knitting loom. Loom knitting patterns range from simple hats and scarves to toys, baby items, bags, sweaters, socks, and much more.

From free loom knitting patterns for babies, to wearables and decor, some of the loom knitting patterns you'll find in this list include:

- Blankets
- Shawls
- Socks
- Hats
- Baby gifts
- Bags
- Sweaters

and more!

Loom and other

loom knitting

So you want to learn how to loom knit and you are wondering where to start. Well the best place to begin is with the loom itself. Because if you want to loom then you are going to, of course, need a loom...

When it comes to knitting looms on the market today there are hundreds, if not thousands, for the loom knitting enthusiast to choose from! But, what loom is best for you? Well, realistically that all depends on the knitting project and the yarn that you want to use. As a beginner to loom knitting, I would suggest that you start off with either a set of round or long looms. Another loom option that is good for beginners as well, is the basic loom which is used to teach loom knitting. The slideshow above pictures several popular types of looms on the market today. Which include the following:
Round Loom Set, Long Loom Set, Rainbow Loom, Spool loom, Sock Loom, Flower loom, Hat loom, Scarf Loom, Afghan loom, and the Zippy Loom!

Other Supplies You'll Need
Besides your knitting loom, you'll also need to gather the following supplies to create your loom knitting project:
- Yarn
- Loom tool (sometimes called a loom hook)
- Tapestry needles
- Scissors
- Other notions (buttons, pompoms, etc.)

Yarn

Be The Boss

To have full control over your weaving, you need to know how the fibers work with each other.
Wool, cotton, rayon, silk, polyester, and acrylic each have their own personality, and a good weaver knows how to make them get along.
You also need to know which fiber is best suited to your project.
So let's get started!
I'll describe each fiber, its characteristics, and how I like to use it.

1. Fibers from Animals

We call the fibers from animals protein fibers. You especially need to know this when you're dyeing the yarn. Protein fibers need different dyesthan plant fibers.

Wool

Wool is the most forgiving fiber, and it's easy to work with. It packs down beautifully, and with its slight stretch, is forgiving.

Most wool we use is spun after the fibers have been carded and fluffed up, creating the soft, cozy yarns we use in clothing and rugs.

Another type of wool yarn is called worsted, in which the fibers are not carded, but combed and spun into a dense yarn. These yarns are usually used in coats, rugs, and upholstery, and are expensive.

I live in the desert, and don't wear wool much. I use it mostly in rugs and in my coiled baskets.

Wool needs special care, you can't just throw it in the washer and dryer or it will shrink. I always say to treat it like you would yourself.

Don't toss it in a tub of hot water. Would you like that? Treat it gently, and start with lukewarm water, water that you'd like to jump into for a nice soothing bath. Don't squish it or handle it too much, or the tiny microscopic scales on the wool fibers will bind together and "felt-up."

On the other hand, sometimes you do want it to turn into felt, and that's the subject for another post!

Silk

Well, silk is silky! Its lustrous sheen is perfect for scarves, and it drapes so beautifully.

When you weave with silk, you'll find it slips around a bit, so it's a good idea to keep the weave dense, an airy weave might just turn into a mess when you wear it and wash it. Above you see a photo of some silk chenille that I hand-dyed. Silk chenille... now that was a treat for me to buy because it's expensive! I used it in some tiny amulet necklaces (Amulets are little bags from ancient times, people kept special treasures in them). Beside the chenille is some red and blue skeins of tussah silk.

There's another kind of silk that has a more organic, earthy feel. It's called raw silk. The photo above is raw silk. It's not as slinky as regular silk, but I love its organic feel, and it drapes well.

Raw silk is made from the outer part of the silk cocoon and has a slightly sticky feel with tiny bits of organic stuff.

I like to use both kinds of silk, but since I'm a granola-eater girl, and I am not rich, I often use raw silk in the clothes I make.

There are other kinds of animal fibers, yak, camel, alpaca, llama, and rabbit. Actually, any animal hair can be spun into yarn if you've a mind to do it. I've got a sweater with my first dog's fur knitted in. When I wear it, I think of sweet Mava.

2. Fibers from Plants

Plant fibers are called cellulose fibers. These, like the protein fibers, require dyes meant to be absorbed into the cellulose structure.

Cotton

Cotton is my favorite, it's soft, absorbent, and easy to weave. It usually costs less than wool or silk.
It comes in many grades, from simple cotton twine to silky, lustrous yarn.
Mercerized cotton has been treated to make the yarn have more luster and dyes well.
Unmercerized cotton is not as vibrant and is good for towels because it is more absorbent.

Linen

Linen is made from flax, and unlike cotton, its fibers come from the stalk of the plant. It's called a bast fiber.

Linen can be tricky to weave with because it doesn't stretch. A little stretch in a fiber allows us to tweak the tension on the loom and forgives us when we don't wind the yarn on perfectly.

But I love linen, it smells so nice, you feel like you're outside on a spring day. Linen is also a bit pricey, so a nice alternative to pure linen is Cottolin. Cottolin is 60% cotton and 40% linen. The cotton makes it easier to work with, less expensive, and it has the same sweet fragrance.

Hemp

Hemp is also a bast fiber, and stiff to work with. I've not used it for weaving… but I soon will! I ordered too much hemp twine for my packaging, so I'm going to give it a try to make some placemats.

Hemp isn't the same grade as linen, not as lustrous, and its fibers are shorter. It's strong and a great fiber for baskets.

Rayon

Rayon is a sorta natural fiber. By sorta I mean that it is made from cellulose, but it's manufactured with polymers, so that makes it sorta natural.

Rayon is made from wood pulp then put through spinnerets, much like the silkworm does when making its cocoon. Find out more here.

I love working with rayon, it feels natural, drapes like silk, and the sheen is almost the same as silk too.

Soy

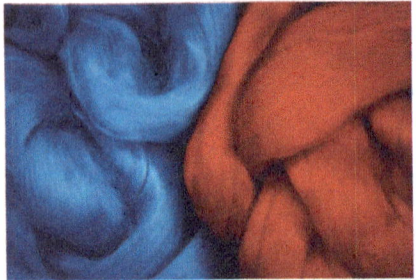

There are a lot of different fibers coming out as eco-friendly, and soyis the most popular with weavers. It drapes even more beautifully than rayon and dyes up into vibrant colors. It's often blended with silk and cotton.

I can't tell you a lot about it because I haven't used it yet, I just bought some beautiful soy roving at a wool festival, and I'll probably just swoon over it for a while, then put it into something I'm felting.

3. Synthetic Fibers

Acrylic

I'll just get the truth out right now.

I don't like to weave with acrylic. It's got too much static, and just isn't fun to weave with.

But I don't like acrylic anything. It doesn't let your skin breath. Natural fibers always feel much nicer to the skin.

It's dependable because you always know that it won't shrink or change much in the washing process.

You can buy some very nice acrylic, and there are lots of high-end blends, so don't pass it up if you see something you just love.

Polyester and nylon are also blended into yarns. They give it strength, luster, and are usually found in novelty yarns.

Novelty yarns have all kinds of fun, bumpy, furry, and shiny things added in.

Metallic

Metallics are nice to add a little sparkle to your handwoven fabric, and a little goes a long way. I used this one for just a few rows in some placemats.

Loom

Introduction to Loom Knitting

Why Loom Knit?

Loom knitting creates a very even knit fabric similar to needle knitting, but the process is different and, incredibly easy to learn. Make beautiful knitwear like hats, scarves, cowls, shawls, blankets, sweaters and much more with a simple wrap and hook process. A great benefit of loom knitting is that it's gentle on wrists and hands and can be faster than knitting needles, especially with double knitting. Also, it's easy to see your stitches, and keep track of your knitting.

Types of Knitting Looms

Knitting looms are designed to work in single knit and/or double knit. In single knitting, you are creating a knitted piece that looks similar to needle knit. Knitting in flat panel, for projects like scarves, blankets, and shawls, any knitting loom can be used. But single knitting, in the round (tubular shape) for items like hats, cowls, and socks requires a round loom with a set number of pegs.

In double knitting, the knit is created on a long loom/knitting board or with the 'Rotating' Double Knit Loom. This requires 2 rows of pegs with an opening in between them. Yarn is wrapped across the loom to utilize both rows of pegs to interlock the stitches, and create a double-sided fabric. There is no backside. Double knitting is a great method when you want to put designs in your work.

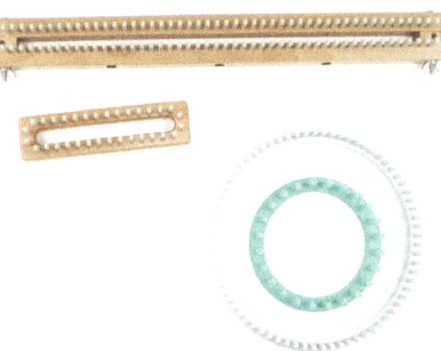

What Knitting Loom is Best?

Knitting looms come in various shapes and sizes. There are round looms, long looms/ knitting boards, adjustable looms (work as both a round and long loom) and modular looms (you customize with the pegs you need). Choose your loom based on what you would like to create.

Just like in needle knitting, where needles come in different sizes to create different size stitches, looms have the same options. Looms come in a variety of gauges depending on what size stitch you would like to create; fine, small, regular, and chunky gauge. The smaller gauges have thinner pegs with less space between the pegs, and usually use a thinner yarn. The spacing from center of one peg to the center of adjacent peg determines your knitting gauge. Looms with wider spacing between the pegs accommodates thicker yarns, and thus creates larger gauges.

For Beginners a great place to start is with large gauge looms (large pegs), as it is easier to see stitches, and faster to knit. You may consider the Zippy Loom (very large pegs), Flexee Loom Chunky, or Chunky Round Loom Set. For double knitting, start with the simple Basic Loom, or the super versatile All-n-One Loom.

Knitting Loom Options

Round Loom Sets
Round Looms Chunky (large gauge), Round Looms (small gauge), Baby Knit Looms (small gauge).
These knitting loom sets are great for hats, scarves, socks, slippers and other small projects. Each of the looms have a stationary number of pegs which means you can knit one size per loom.

Knitting Looms for Large Projects

Large projects like shawls, blankets, or sweaters, use a loom with at least 100 – 200+ pegs. The best knitting looms for single knit blankets are the Afghan Loom, Multi-Knit Loom, or Flexee Loom (add any number of pegs). For blankets in both single and double knit, an adjustable loom is recommended, 18" All-n-One Loom, 28" Loom or 38" Loom.
Modular Knitting Looms
These knitting looms give you the most flexibility with single knitting in creating various size round looms. The Multi-Knit Loom allows you to snap together parts and create over 18 different configurations. If you want to custom create looms based on each project, the brand new Flexee Loom Links is recommended. It's a set of (2) peg links that easily connect and allow you to build any size knitting loom. With additional kits, connect more links... the possibilities are endless.

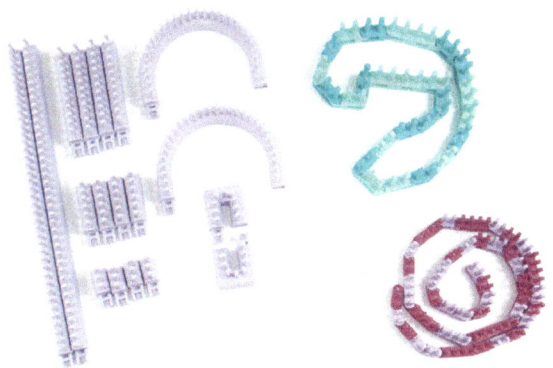

Double Knitting Looms

The All-n-One Loom, 28" Loom, 38" Loom, and the 'Rotating' Double Knit Loom all work in both double knit and single knit. For small projects, specifically double-knit hats, the 'Rotating' Double Knit Loom is best to create the tubular shape without any sewing.

Sock Looms

These small looms are ideal for knitting socks, but can knit a variety of other small projects, as well. The Sock Loom Original (fine gauge), and Sock Loom 2 (regular gauge) are both adjustable for any size sock. The stationary, (2) sock loom set, His & Her Sock Looms, works really well for adult size socks.

Other tools

WHAT YOU NEED FOR YOUR LOOM KNITTING PATTERNS

I know you're itching to try out loom knit patterns, but we need to talk briefly about some of the important tools and materials you will need to complete a loom knit project.

- Loom hooks – Loom hooks are used to create the stitches in loom knitting. These are tools that have a pointed tip at an angle so you can grab the loops of yarn and hook it over the peg to make a new stitch.
- Scissors – A pair of scissors is another important tool that you will use for all of your knitting projects. You'll need them to cut the yarn when you're done!
- Stitch markers – You might need stitch markers to keep track of where you are if you're following a stitch pattern. If you don't have stitch markers, you can use a strand of scrap yarn—preferably in a different color so it's easy to see.
- Yarn/darning needle – You will need a yarn needle or darning needle to sew in the loose ends.

Information for beginner

Your favourite knitting stitches can be created on your loom according to how you wrap the yarn around the pegs. Different wrapping techniques will produce different textures and designs to produce satisfyingly plush projects from traditional stitches to more intricate styles including lace or cablework. Anything is possible with a loom and a little know-how!

It's important to bear in mind often loom knitting stitches have different names to those created by needles.

HOW TO USE A KNITTING LOOM

Knitting looms come in a variety of shapes and sizes depending on what kind of project you are making. While long looms work best for projects like scarves, round (or circular) looms are best for hats, socks or anything that has a tube structure.

BASE, PEGS AND GAUGE

Let's get down to basics. The anatomy of a loom is made up of three essential components; base, pegs and gauge. The base is the frame at the bottom of your loom which might be a long or round available in lots of sizes. The pegs describe the multiple short pins attached to the base - sometimes these are just called pins. The gauge is the distance between each peg (or pin), the wider the gap is between the pegs the greater the gauge. Easy-peasy!

SO WHAT DETERMINES THE SIZE OF YOUR PROJECT?

The size of your project can be affected by many things, the first is the size of your loom. Many fledgling loom knitters refer to the size of the loom as the number of pegs, but this is a massive no-no! As a beginner it's important to remember that it's actually the size of the base that determines the size of your project, not necessarily the number of pegs. The number of pegs and the gauge influence the tension of your stitches, or how tightly knit together your stitches are. More pegs does not necessarily mean a bigger size.

Saying that, there is one exception - and that is the style of stitch. If you use a loose stitch such as an Ewrap stitch then your fabric will be looser and therefore be a slightly bigger size then if you were to use a garter stitch on your loom.

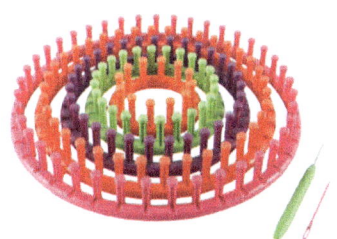

ROW VS PEG COUNT

When it comes to the number of rows and pegs on your loom knitting project, it's important to remember that these are not interchangeable. The peg count determines the circumference or width of your project, and the number of rows is how many times you repeat this. If you are making a tubular project such as socks or a hat on a round loom, then the rows will only add to the length of the tube, but not give anymore give around the foot or head.

In addition to your loom and yarn you will also need a hook to catch and pull your loops of yarn over to create the knitted stitches.

LOOM KNITTING STITCHES

Just like knitting with needles, loom knitting includes a whole encyclopedia of stitches to craft beautifully textured knitwear.

Before we get to specific stitches, there are two fundamental methods of knitting on a loom: single and double knitting.

SINGLE KNITTING

Single-knitting is when you knit stitches on pegs next to one another, creating a fabric which will have a 'right' and 'wrong' side.

KNIT STITCH (K)

The knit stitch on a loom has the very same texture and look as a knit stitch created using regular needles. The knit stitch is achieved by using your hook to pull at the yarn looped around your peg, to create a new loop. By lifting the old loop up and over, you replace with the new loop on your peg to create a new knit stitch. And that's it!

This is the primal stitch that once mastered can be combined with purl to create garter stitch or even ribbed stitches.

FLAT STITCH (F)

Flat stitch is a close cousin of knit stitch, except it's tighter more compact. Stretch the working yarn across the top loop of the peg and simply use your hook to lift the bottom loop over and off your peg, securing the working yarn in place by making it a new loop.

PURL STITCH (P)

Just like in traditional knitting, the purl stitch is the reverse of the knit stitch, meaning that the backside of your fabric will be knit material the frontside will be purl. Both knit and purl stitches are fantastic starting points to launch you into a world of glorious textures and designs as you learn to loom knit.

DOUBLE KNITTING

Double-knitting is when you knit across two rails, if you are using a long loom, so you have a front and a back peg, meaning you get the same texture on both sides of your fabric.

NO WRAP STITCH (NW)

In loom knitting this might be referred to as a flat (stockinette) stitch, and when knitting with needles this is known as the basic knit stitch (k). Just like the gorgeous basic fabric produced when knitting with needles, the no wrap stitch creates sturdy yet beautifully adaptable material which can be transformed into fabulous accessories and homeware. As one of the most basic stitches, the no wrap stitch is a staple for the avid loom knitter and can be used on a long loom or round one. And that's a wrap!

EWRAP (EW)

Better known as the twisted stockinette stitch when knitting with needles (tw St st), the ewrap works a treat on both long and round looms.

SINGLE RIBBED STITCH OR RIBBING STITCH (RIB)

Perfect for gloves and garments with the iconic ribbed effect, the single ribbed stitch sees ewrap stitches alternate with purl stitches on each row creating glorious ridges of yarn.

Loom Knitting Patterns

Pumpkins

Love the look of knitting things but don't know how to knit? Check out these gorgeous LOOM KNIT pumpkins that are a breeze to whip up!

Luckily earlier this year I had already tackled my yarn stash and I've got tubs divided out by weight and color. And when I realized that I have an entire tub of remnant Hometown USA yarn balls I decided to put some of them to good use.

I brought in a ball of my favorite mustard color and started to crochet up a pumpkin. But I thought, I totally did that last year. I also have a tub full of my knitting looms. And so I went back out, grabbed a medium sized loom for chunky yarn and got after it.

Sitting on my sofa I also had a little stash of felt from another project I'd been working on while couch surfing. And so my little pumpkin stems were born out of the brown felt from that little photo box and even if chosen out of convenience, I don't think I could love any other DIY stem option more. Today I'm going to show you just how easy it is to make these pumpkins. Once you get going you can get one done, start to finish in about an hour. And if you're a brand new loom knitter… no sweat. I'll show you each and every step to make your own loom knit pumpkins.

This is a long ride… ready to tuck in?

TOOLS NEEDED TO MAKE PUMPKINS ON A KNITTING LOOM:

- Chunky Yarn Round Knitting Loom
- Loom Knitting Hook
- 3.75" Yarn Needles
- Embroidery Needle
- Scissors

My loom knit pumpkins were made using a knitting loom specifically sized for weight 5, bulky yarn. There are also looms for thinner medium weight yarns (e.g. Red Heart Super Saver Yarn). When side by side, you can tell the difference in loom by the size of the pegs. The thinner pegs are used for thinner yarns. Both will work well to knit up some pumpkins but the chunkier yarn will yield results much more quickly. I was able to knit 5 different bulky yarn pumpkins in less time than 1 pumpkin using medium yarn pumpkins. In fact, I haven't quite finished that one, yet! :)

Be sure to use the right
sized loom for your yarn.

To finish your pumpkins
you'll need yarn needles. I
really, really recommend
these 3.75" Boye Yarn
Needles because they are
the longest I can find with
a dull end and will easy go
all of the way through even a fat yarn pumpkin.

Supplies Needed to Make Pumpkins on a Knitting Loom:
- Bulky Yarn
- Brown Felt
- Brown Embroidery Floss
- Poly-Fil

Even if a yarn says that it is a Weight 5 Bulky yarn on the
packaging, not all will be exactly the same. I found that Lion
Brand Hometown USA and Lion Brand Wool Ease Thick &
Quick worked the best for loom knit pumpkins. I tried other
brands, including Michael's Charisma, which is also listed as
a Weight 5 Bulky. The Charisma was much thinner than the
Lion Brand yarns and yielded huge gaps in the knit, which I
wasn't happy about. If using a brand other than
recommended, I'd suggest buying one skein and making
sure you're happy with the knit before committing to a full
shopping basket of bulky yarn.

FIRST, LET'S COVER THE BASIC HOW TO FOR E-WRAP KNITTING ON A ROUND LOOM:

There is a peg on the side of your loom. Making a simple, overhanded knot, tie the yarn to this peg.

Wrap the yarn around the first peg in line with your tied knot in a clockwise fashion.

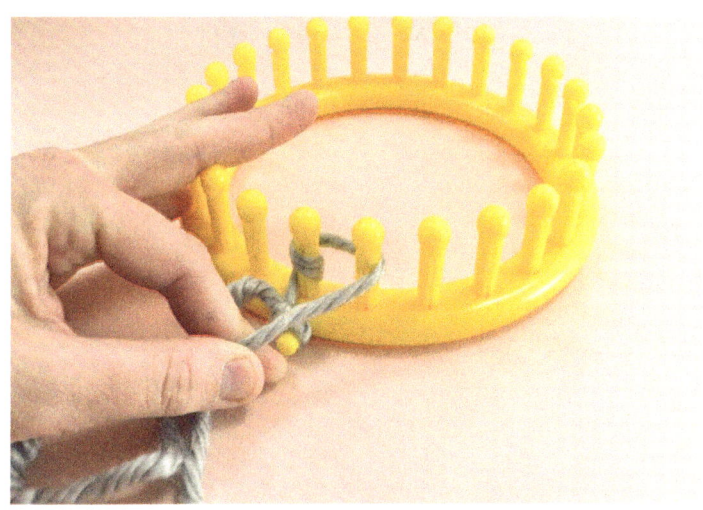

Wrap around the next peg, and each peg around in a clock-wise. Be sure that the wrap is tight enough that the yarn stays where you wrap it high on the peg and does not droop down to the base of the loom. You don't want the yarn to get too tight, though, as it will make knitting difficult. If you're brand new to loom knitting, this might take a few turns around the loom before you find the right tension for your wraps.

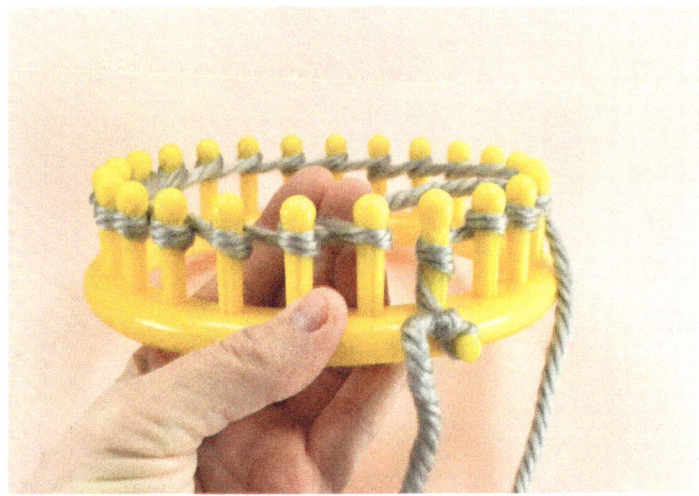

Stop wrapping when you get to the last peg on the loom.

Holding your last wrap in place, push the yarn to the base of the loom on all pegs.

Repeat the wrapping process, running your yarn around clockwise for each peg, starting with the first (right above the knot on the side of the loom).

Holding the last wrap in place, put the loom knitting tool inside of the last peg's groove. Pull the tool upward to hook the yarn.

Pull the bottom loop over the top loop leaving the top loop in place on the peg.

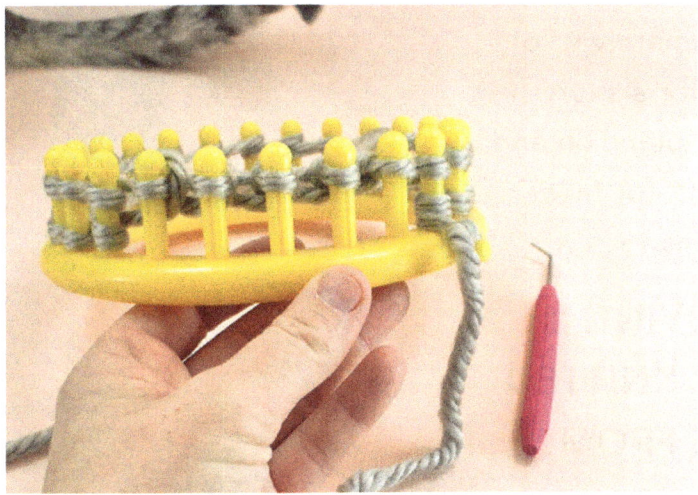

Continue pulling the bottom loops over the top and off of the peg for around, working counter-clockwise until you return to the first peg.

When you've taken off all of the loops, repeat the knitting process… Push the loops on the pegs down to the loom's base. Wrap the yarn around each peg until you reach the last. Holding the last loop in place, hook the bottom loop with your tool and pull over the the top loop and off of the peg. Continue until you knit approximately 6" of length for a short, squatty pumpkin and up to 10" for taller pumpkins.

REMOVING YOUR KNITTED PIECE FROM THE LOOM:

Cut your yarn from the skein leaving a tail of 18-24″. This tail will be used to create the segments of the pumpkin a little later on. Thread the end of your tail through the eye of your long yarn needle.

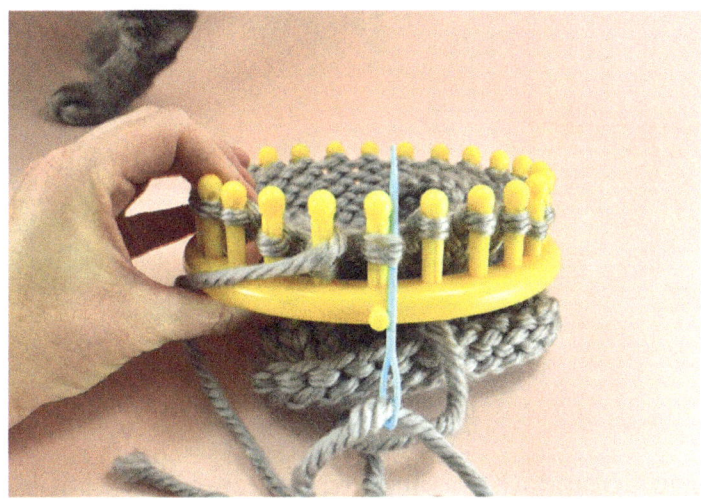

Push the tip of your needle into the first peg's groove and push the needle beneath the loop on the peg. Pull the needle all of the way through the loop. Continue pulling your threaded needle through all of the loops on all of the pegs.

Quick Tip – If the loop tries to slip off of the loom, hold it in place with one hand while pulling your needle through with the other.

Use your loom knitting tool to pull all of the loops off of the loom.

CREATING FELT STEMS FOR YOUR LOOM KNIT PUMPKINS:

From a piece of brown felt cut a circle approximately the size of a quarter and a rectangle that measures 2" x 3.5". Thread and embroidery needle with matching floss.

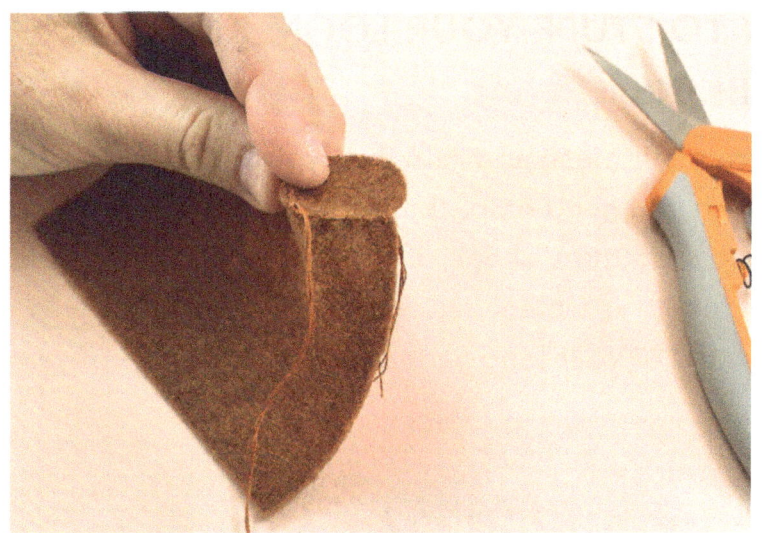

Using the blanket stitch, sew together the round and long side of the rectangle pieces to form a stem.

When you get to the point where the felt will overlap itself round the stem, trim the excess. Stitch together the gap to the bottom of the stem. Leave a tail of embroidery floss of 6-8".

HOW TO STUFF YOUR LOOM KNIT PUMPKINS:

Take your knit piece and turn it so you are working with the bottom. If you need help, the bottom has the starting tail (shorter). Also the V shape of the stitches will point toward the bottom of the piece.

Thread one of your long yarn needles with 8-10" of yarn.

The bottom of your knit piece will have a loop on each stitch that is naturally looser than any other stitches in

the whole piece. Run your threaded yarn needle up and through each of these loose loops for each stitch all of the way around the base. Always bring the needle up underneath the loop and through before passing onto the next.

Once you've run the yarn through all loops remove the needle. Pull both ends of the yarn piece tight to close the bottom of the loom knit pumpkin like a drawstring bag. Push the tails in through the hole into the inside of the pumpkin. Pull both strings as tight as you can to close up the cinch as much as possible. Tie both ends of the yarn into 2 overhand knots to secure. Leave the tails inside of the pumpkin.

Fill the inside of the pumpkin with Poly-Fil until approximately 3/4 full.
Note – the more you stuff the pumpkins the more spread out your stitches will be and the more visible the filling inside.

Begin pulling the tail at the top of the pumpkin to begin closing the hole. Place the stem into the hole and pull the yarn tightly for a secure fit. It might be necessary to finagle the pleats around the stem for a neat look.

Re-thread your embroidery needle with the tail from your stem. Use it to stitch through the yarn into the stem and out of the other side to secure the stem to the pumpkin.

Push the needle through the interior of the pumpkin and out of the side or bottom. Pull the thread taut and trim. The tail will get lost inside of the pumpkin's stuffing.

CREATING SEGMENTS IN YOUR LOOM KNIT PUMPKINS:

If necessary rethread the tail around the pumpkin's stem into a yarn needle.

Push the threaded needle down in through the center of the

pumpkin and out of the center of the bottom. (This is when these long 3.75" yarn needles come in crazy handy!)

To create your first segment push the yarn needle into the pumpkin where you'd like the segment to run. (For your first segment it doesn't matter where you start, but needle placement will matter for your following stitches).
Pull the needle all of the way through the bottom center of the pumpkin but leave the stitch loose.

The segment will occur where this stitch is tightened. Make sure this running segment is nice and straight.

Pull the stitch tight to form your first segment.

Push the needle through the top along the stem where you'd like your next segment to be through the bottom. Pull the stitch tight to form the segment. Repeat until your pumpkin has enough sections.

Quick tip – Last year I hooked up some crochet pumpkins that were very symmetrical. This year I wanted a kind of wonky pumpkin akin to an heirloom tomato. For my odd shapes and segments I varied pulling the stitches loosely through to very tightly through. If you would prefer a more symmetrical look, make all of your stitches using even tension.

To finish your pumpkin make a few small stitches at the bottom center to secure. Run the needle up through the inside of the pumpkin and out of the side. Pull the yarn taut and snip close.

a Cap - E - Wrap Method

Learn how to loom knit a hat with this easy tutorial!

I am highly impressionable. What can I say? I get teased tons because even though I worked in marketing, was really good at my job and totally understood how and why commercials and product placement in stores worked, I STILL am a sucker for good marketing. I don't watch much TV and that's probably a good thing.

I set up the bunny ears running cords over to the window to watch election coverage hooha. Any time a commercial came on one I would suddenly feel the need for a soda or decide I wanted to go out to eat even though my dinner was still digesting in my belly. I am the exact type of person that commercials are made for... highly impressionable and easily swayed :)

But out of the blue, I got this set of round looms to knit on. To be honest I didn't know much about them but I grabbed some Lion Brand Hometown USA bulky yarn and got to it. The next day I was up at the store stocking up on various colors of this fab yarn because I was hooked. I have to tell you that I have made a RIDICULOUS amount of hats and I've also got to tell you IT'S SO STINKING EASY! And last, but not least, they look properly knitted. It's not like a crochet stitch that can kind of pass for knitting, it's properly knitting just in a different format. Seriously, y'all... since that very first cap I'm in love.

So today I'm going to show you how to loom knit a hat. All you need is a large round loom and some bulky yarn. It's so very simple that chances are your very first attempt will be perfectly wearable, too. Huzzah!

For this project you will need:

- Large round loom (I use a Boye set)
- Loom hook (comes with the set)
- Bulky yarn

You can make an adult size hat using one skein of Hometown USA. This includes a pompom if you're so inclined.

This is the largest loom from my Boye loom kit and the loom hook that comes with it.

Now to start, and to totally keep things real my yarn started out as a disaster. I pulled the center piece of yarn and out came this nightmare. Ugh but it's hardly the end of the world, right?!? :)

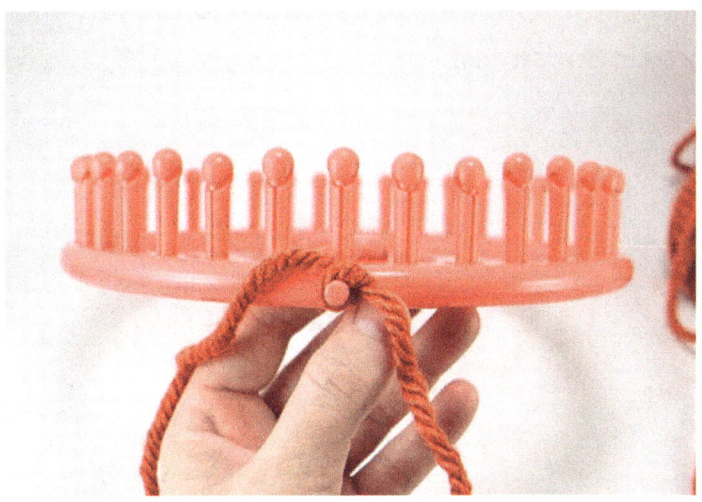

To start, tie an overhand knot onto the peg on the side of your loom. It doesn't need to be crazy tight. This is just to keep our yarn from getting away from us as we start the looming process.

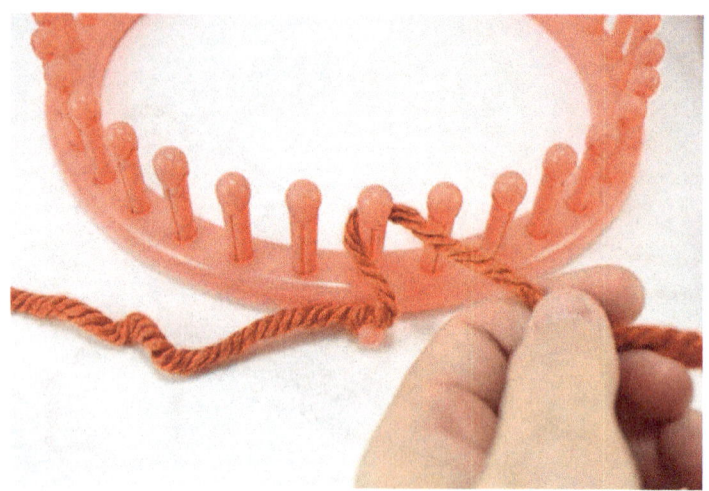

You're going to take the working yarn (the long bit as it comes out of your skein) to the right of the loom and wrap it around every peg in a clockwise fashion. Be sure to start with the peg just about your side peg. This will help with a visual cue to remember which peg is the first one.

*sidenote: If left-handed you can work to the left and wrap in a counter-clockwise fashion.

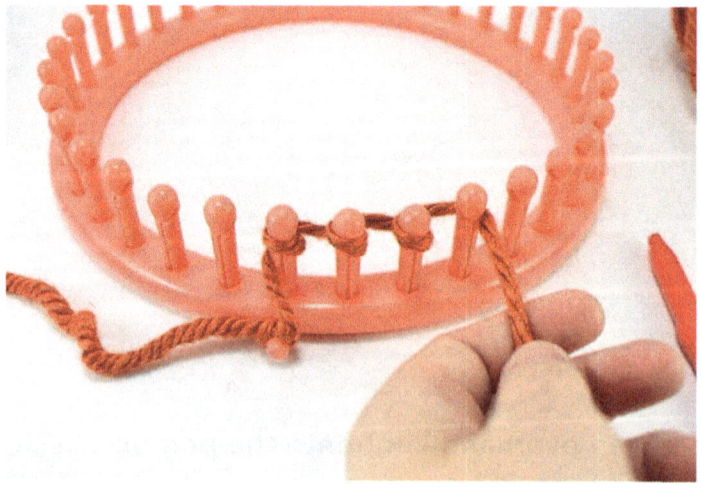

As you loop your yarn around each peg it is very, very important to keep the yarn nice and loose. Too tight and working the yarn later is a nightmare. Just keep it nice and loose as you go.

FYI – this is the E-wrap method, because you wrap the yarn around each peg in a lower-case "e" shape as it goes around each peg clock-wise.

Now in case you're one of those crafters where the more details you have about the process the better, this tip is for you :) This is the inside of my loom. This is how the yarn should look from the inside if it is properly wrapped.

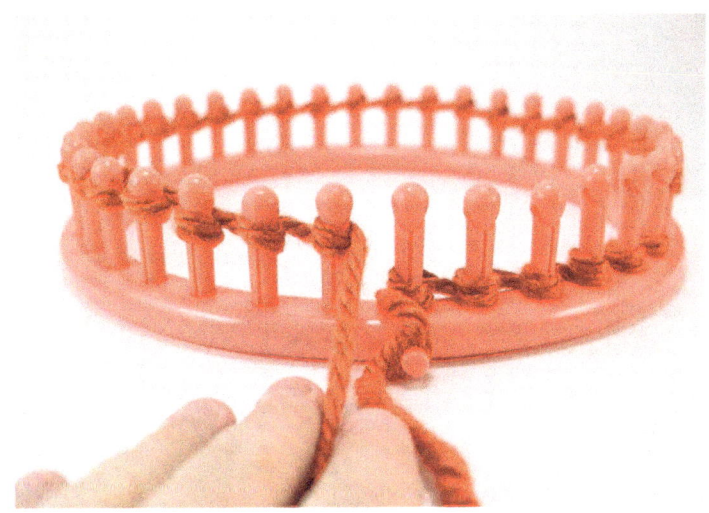

Wrap all of the way to the last peg.
Holding on to your yarn so that it doesn't get away from you, push the yarn down to the bottom of each peg, all of the way around.

Wrap your yarn, loosely and counter-clockwise again around all of the pegs. Hang onto that yarn because the moment you let go that yarn will unwind off of those pegs like the dickens!

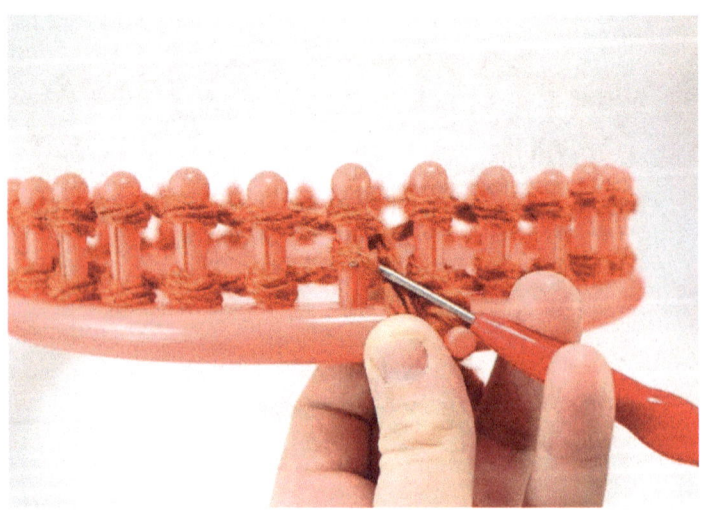

Using your loom hook grab the bottom loop on the LAST peg you wrapped.

Pull that loop up and over the peg.

Continue pulling the bottom loops over the pegs all of the way around.

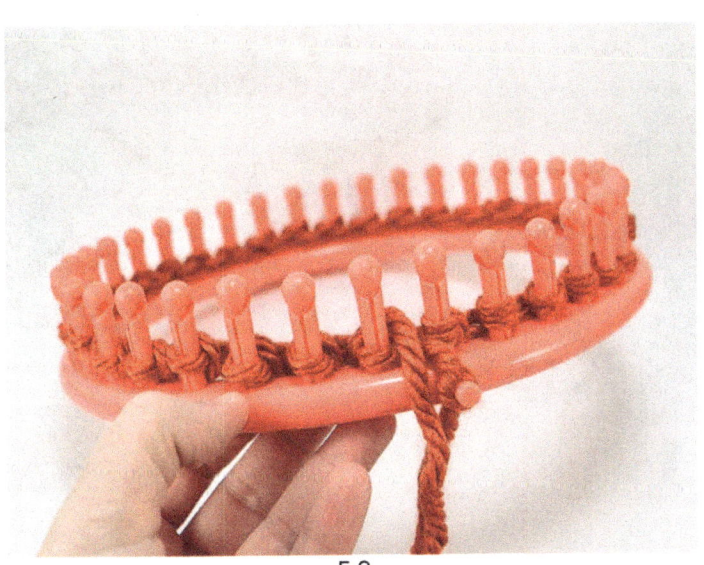

Push your yarn to the bottom of each peg, all of the way around.

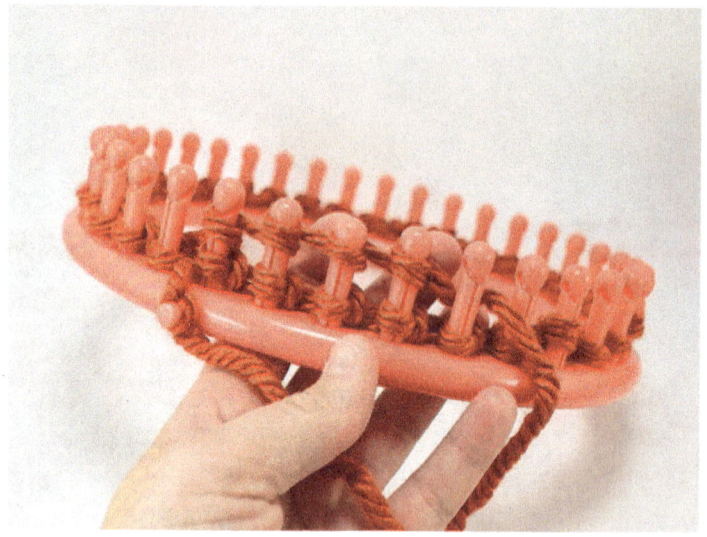

Continue the knitting process. *Wrap the yarn clockwise, loosely around each peg. Starting with the last peg wrapped pull the bottom loop up and off of the peg. Continue around the loom. Push the yarn to the bottom of each peg. Repeat from *.

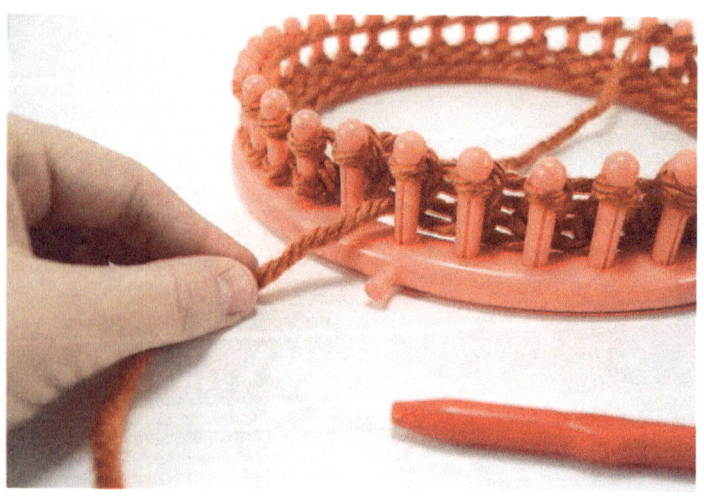

Once you get a few rows of knitting done you'll need to untie the tail from the side peg. If you leave the tail it messes with the tension and your rows get all strange.

Knit around and around until you reach a length of 10 inches for a tighter fit knit hat. Add more length for a knit slouch beanie.

Cut your working yarn to 24-32 inches long and thread through a yarn needle (comes with your kit).

Push your need up through every loop on every peg, starting with the first (just above the side peg) and all the way around.

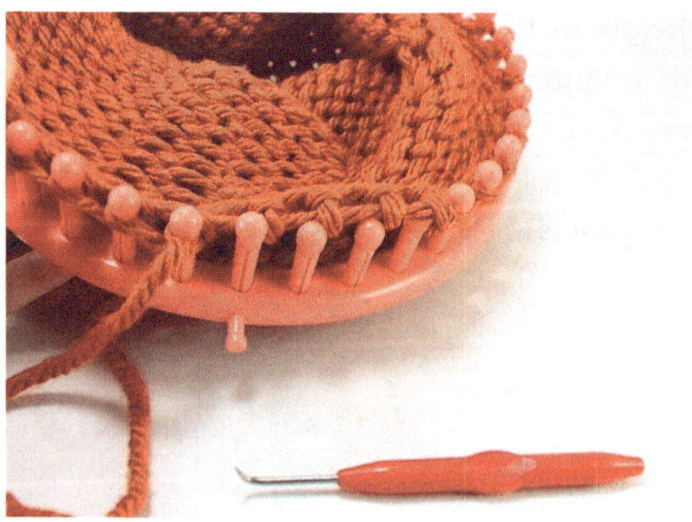

Once you've connected all of the loops on all of the pegs you can begin removing them with your loom hook.

This is the knit piece as it looks straight off of the loom.

Pull the tail of the yarn tight to pucker the piece and form the top of the cap. Take care to pleat and tuck as you tighten to make sure the top looks neat.

Make several stitches to keep the tightened area together.
Finish by running your needle and yarn inside of the cap.

Weave in the ends and trim the excess yarn away.
Add a pompom if you please. This is actually a faux fur pom I
got on sale at Michael's. Isn't it fun?

I have been bitten majorly hard with the loom knitting bug. Every once in a while this thing happens where I try a new (or new to me) craft and fall head over heels purchasing absolutely everything I might ever need that has anything to do with my new craft/hobby.

Still with me? Good! Let's get after it. For this project you will need:

- Bulky yarn knitting loom (I love my Boye set)
- Hometown USA yarn (equivalent to 1 skein) – get it for around $3 apiece at Walmart, seriously the cheapest price I have found...

Get after loom knitting your cap as you would anyway. It's time to switch business up when you have 6-8 inches of length knitted up (more or less depending on the size of your brim, I suppose).

Follow down the knit from the loop on the peg to the end of the piece. Grab that loop at the end and pull it over that peg.

Working to the left, or right, continue bringing the matching bottom loop up placing it onto the peg.

This is what your piece will look like when all of the ends have been matched up. This is your brim where the knit is doubled up making it warmer and visibly thicker when worn.

To wrap this brim up bring the bottom loop over the peg, just as you would normally knit.

After that just continue knitting as you please!
I really love how making a brim is a thicker piece since it's doubled over. That added thickness makes for an awesome look. It also eliminates how the bottom of knit caps like to roll up like the one I made below.

The brim also adds extra warmth with 2 layers instead of just the 1 and it also adds more protection against the wind which is perfect for anyone who suffers frequent earaches.
So there you have it. Easy peasy loom knit hats with a brim!

Dewdrop Washcloth Makes

Washcloths make a quick, easy and economical addition to include in a spa set, bridal shower gift or a "just because" for a good friend. But they can be a bit boring.

Sure garter stitch is easy, but it's just so, so... garter-y. (Yup, I'm making up words here.) Washcloths are the perfect size for trying out new stitch patterns. They're just big enough to get the hang of the stitch, but you're not stuck working on it for next 65 inches.

It's time to add a little flair to your next washcloth with the dewdrop stitch. This lightly textured stitch makes a beautiful washcloth that is easy to loom knit.

LOOM KNIT DEWDROP STITCH WASHCLOTH PATTERN

MATERIALS

- Yarn: Medium weight (#4) cotton yarn. Premier Yarns Home Cotton in colors Pastel Blue and Cream
- Loom: ⅜" small gauge (SG) loom with at least 37 (43) pegs. Kiss Looms Small Gauge Adjustable loom used in sample.
- Stitch marker
- Tapestry needle

ABBREVIATIONS

k = u-knit stitch

K2tog = knit 2 together

p = purl stitch

sl = slip stitch

yo = yarn over

sk2p = slip 1, knit 2 together, pass the slipped stitch over

ssk = slip, slip, knit

sssk = slip, slip, slip knit

GAUGE

1 repeat (6 sts x 8 rows) = 1.25" x 1.4" in dewdrop stitch pattern

SKILL LEVEL Easy+

MEASUREMENTS

Medium: 8.25" x 8.25" (21 x 21 cm)

Large: 9.5" x 9.5" (24 x 24 cm)

NOTES

Instructions listed are for medium size washcloth.

Adjustments for larger size are listed in parentheses ().

Cast on: I recommend using either the crochet or long tail cast on.

Bind off: I recommend using either the crochet or super stretchy bind off.

Slipped stitch edge: In the video I work Rows 1-7 and slip the first stitch of the row. The chart I included shows the first stitch as knit/purl, but if you prefer to slip those you may.

Chart: The charts are given for the medium size washcloth only. To make the large washcloth work one additional pattern repeat (shown in the red box on the charts).

DEWDROP CLASSIC INSTRUCTIONS

Cast on 37 (43) stitches.

Rows 1-3: p2, *k3, p3. Repeat from * to last 5 sts. k3, p2.

Row 4: ssk, *yo, sssk, yo, k3. Repeat from * to last 2 sts. k2tog

Rows 5-7: k2, *p3, k3. Repeat from * to last 5 sts. p3, k3.

Row 8: ssk, yo, k3, *yo, sssk, yo, k3. Repeat from * to last 2 sts. k2tog.

Repeat Rows 1-8 4 (5) more times. Repeat Rows 1-7 once more.

Bind off and weave in ends.

Classic Dewdrop Washcloth Chart

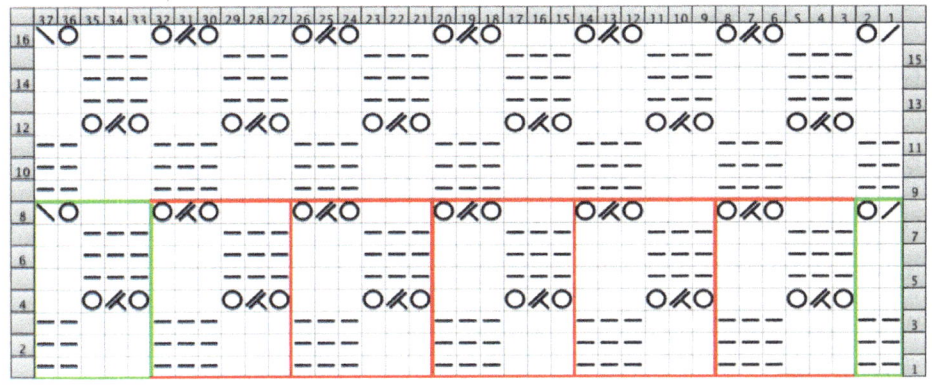

Key

☐	Knit k
╱	Knit 2 Together k2tog
▬	Purl p
╲	Slip Slip Knit ssk
⬈	Slip Slip Slip Knit sssk
◯	Yarn Over yo

DEWDROP VARIATION INSTRUCTIONS

Cast on 37 (43) stitches.

Rows 1-3: sl1, p1, *k3, p3. Repeat from *. End last repeat with p2 instead of p3.

Row 4: sl1, k1, *yo, sk2p, yo, k3. Repeat from *. End last repeat with k2 instead of k3.

Rows 5-7: sl1, k1, *p3, k3. Repeat from *. End last repeat with k2 instead of k3.

Row 8: k2 tog, yo, k3, *yo, sk2p, yo, k3. Repeat from *. End last repeat with k2 (after the final k3).

Repeat Rows 1-8 4 (5) more times. Repeat Rows 1-7 once more.

Bind off and weave in ends.

Variation Dewdrop Washcloth Chart

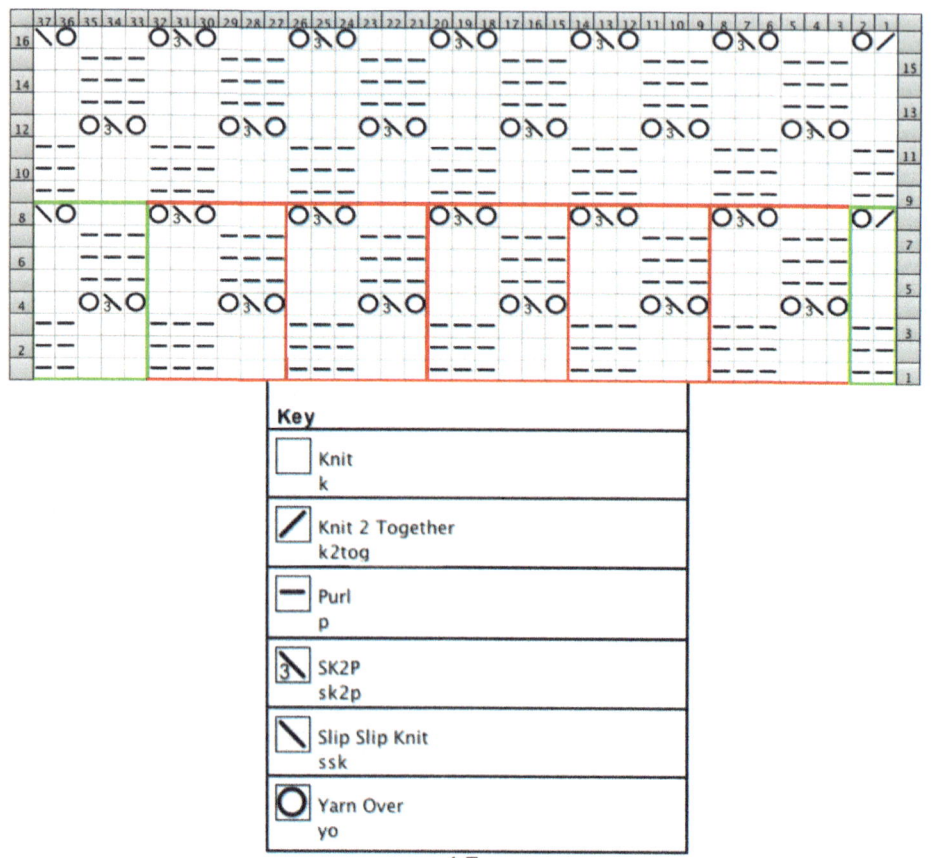

Key

☐	Knit k
◢	Knit 2 Together k2tog
—	Purl p
◣	SK2P sk2p
◥	Slip Slip Knit ssk
◉	Yarn Over yo

Loom Knit Basket

I can't believe that it will be October in just a few short days. If you're like me, you are frantically looking for home-made holiday gift ideas. I designed this sweet little basket with gift-giving in mind. It's a quick loom knit and can be made in a couple of hours. I thought it would be perfect, filled with wrapped Christmas candies and a gift card for a special someone.

Don't forget to make one and keep it for yourself. It would be a great little catch-all basket for your keys and such. Happy looming!-Nicole

If you're like me, you can never have too many baskets. This one will celebrate your love of fiber and act as a cute catch-all!

Level: Beginner

Loom: 40 peg, 3/4" peg spacing, large gauge, round loom.

Finished Measurements: 4"/10.2 cm high x 22"/55.9 cm around. Inside of basket measures 6"/cm across.

Gauge: 8 sts and 20 rows = 4"/10.2 cm square in rib stitch.

Yarn: Lion Brand, Wool-Ease, Thick n' Quick, 79% acrylic, 20% wool, 1% other, 170g/6 oz, 106 yds/96 m.

Color A: 1 skein, #99, Fisherman.

Pattern Notes:
- The main basket is worked in the round from the top down.
- The bottom of the basket is worked in 4 equal wedges and worked flat.
- Alternating e-wrap st and u-knit st gives an interesting texture to the ribbing on this basket.

Pattern

Foundation rnd: Chain CO all pegs with 1 strand color A; join to work in the round.

Rnds 1-3: U-knit

Rnd 4: *U-knit1, p1, rep from * to end of round.

Rnd 5: *Ewk1, p1, rep from * to end of round.

Repeat rnds 4 and 5 until total work measures 4"/10.2 cm.

Begin Bottom Of Basket...

Stop working in the round, work the remainder of the basket flat. Work in sections of ten stitches/pegs. You will have a total of 4 wedges when the basket is complete. If it's helpful use stitch markers to mark the 4 sections.

Row 1: U-knit 10 pegs/sts.(10 sts)

Row 2: Purl 10 pegs/sts.

Row 3: K2tog, u-knit to last 2 sts, ssk. (8 sts)

Row 4: Purl 10 pegs/sts.

Rows 5-8: Repeat rows 3 and 4 (2 times). (4 sts)

Row 9: K2tog, ssk. (2 sts)

Row 10: Purl 2 pegs/sts.

Row 11: K2tog. (1 st)

Bind off 1 stitch/peg cutting working yarn. The section is complete.

Repeat rows 1-11 three more times until you have a total of 4 complete wedges. You will begin working with a new strand of yarn for each wedge (leaving an 8" tail for seaming basket bottom).

Finish: Use garter seaming method to close the bottom of the basket. Weave in all ends. Shape basket, it will take on a natural square shape. This basket does not require blocking.

Hair Scrunchie

If you're looking for a quick last minute gift or you just want to jazz up your hair accessories a bit, some loom knit scrunchies is the perfect project to try.

You can make them in different sizes just by using different types of hair elastics, and you can make them larger or thinner by adding or taking away rows.

It's a super easy, very beginner friendly project and you can have one made in about half an hour.

Loom Knitting Supplies

My favorite way to loom knit is with the large gauge looms. I just love how quickly your project can work up.

For this scrunchie pattern, you'll need a 24 peg loom, which is the smallest one that comes in the Kb large gauge set of round looms.

You'll also need a loom hook (it also comes with the set) and a stitch marker to mark your starting peg.

Best Yarn for Scrunchies

For these cute scrunchies, I used a chenille yarn to make it extra fun and soft.

You could also use a velvet yarn, or really any bulky yarn you like.

I just think using a soft, fuzzy yarn adds to the fun factor for this scrunchie project!

SUPPLIES YOU'LL NEED

- 24 peg large gauge knitting loom
- chenille yarn (size 6) I used Honey Bunny from Hobbii
- hair elastic (whatever type you prefer)
- loom hook
- large eye yarn needle
- stitch marker (to mark first peg)

Step 1: Cast on

First you'll want to place the stitch marker on one of the pegs, and that will be your starting peg.

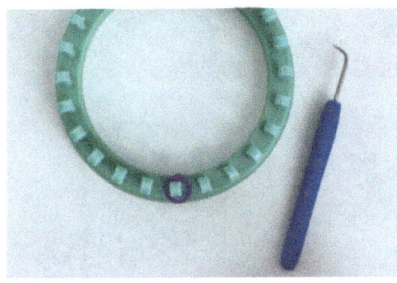

Going to the right, e-wrap around each peg going clockwise around the peg, and continue doing that all the way around the loom.

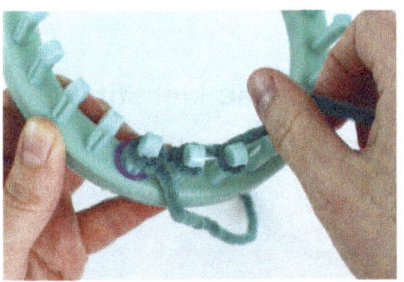

(If your loom has an anchor peg you can skip that, but mine doesn't.)
Take your yarn and make a slip knot, then place the loop from the slip knot onto the first marked peg. Tighten it up.

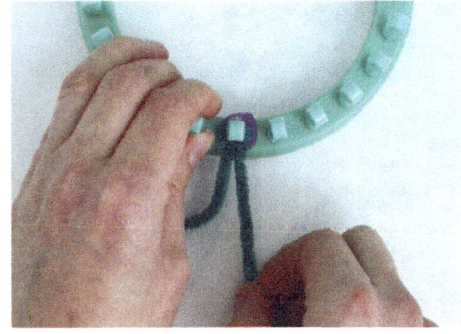

Hold the yarn with one hand so the loops don't come off and push all the loops down to the bottoms of the pegs.

Now we're going to do a
U-wrap cast on.
Wrap the yarn around the
first peg going around in
a counter clockwise
motion.
You're not wrapping all
the way around. Instead
you're just making a "U"
shape (hence the name).

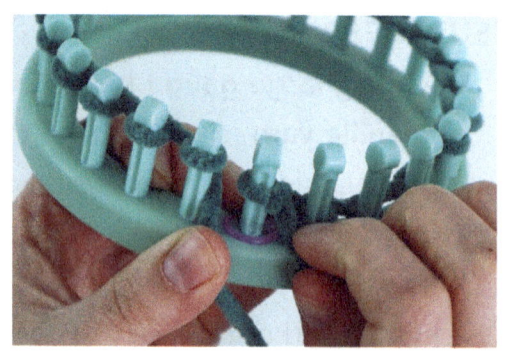

Hold the yarn behind the
peg with one hand while
you pull the bottom loop
over the top loop and off
the peg.

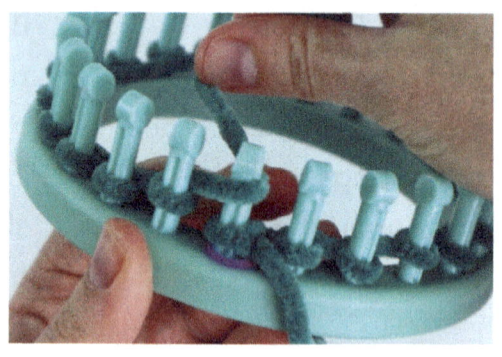

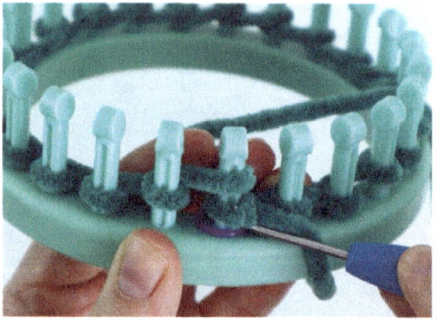
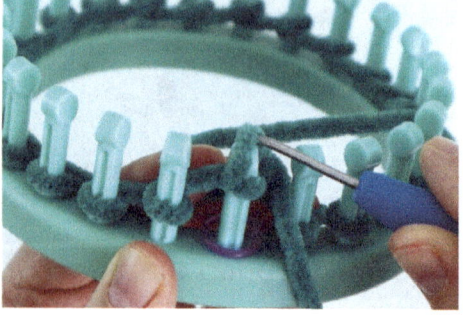

Repeat that with each peg, being careful not to pull too tight
for your U-wraps.

Step 2: Knitting the scrunchie
For the next 15 rows, we'll be doing an E-wrap knit stitch.
To do that, push all the loops on the pegs down to the
bottom.

Then, wrap around each peg in a clockwise motion going to the right until you get all the way around the loom.

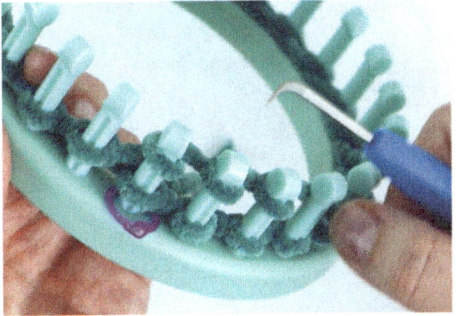
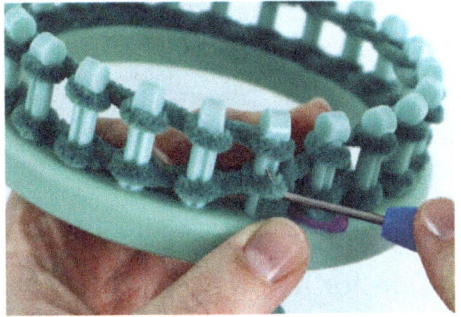

Knit the bottom loop up over and off the last peg you wrapped first (that way it will hold the yarn in place so your loops don't start coming off).

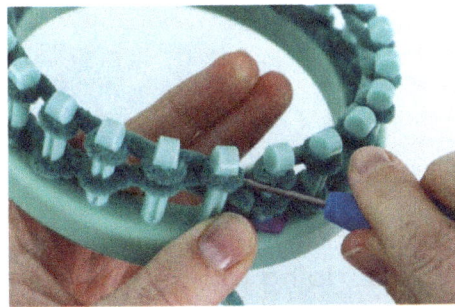

Then continue knitting all the bottom loops over the top loops and off each peg all the way around.

That's one row, and you'll continue doing that until you have e-wrap knitted 15 rows.

Step 3: Folding up the tube
Before we fold up the tube, we're going to go ahead and cut our yarn tail.
Wrap the yarn around the loom 3 times, then cut the yarn.

Thread the yarn onto your yarn needle, and set the needle aside for just a minute.

Set the loom on your desk and pull the tube up through the center of the loom.

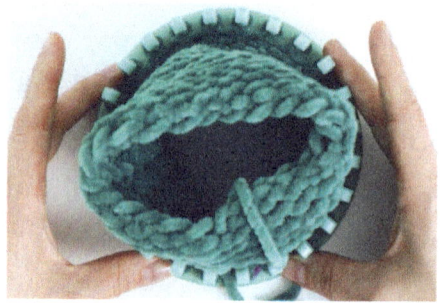
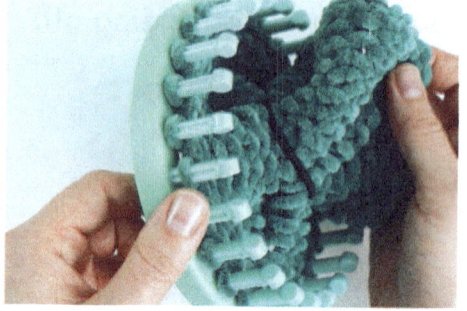

Grab your pony tail holder and you're going to bring the scrunchie tube up through the center of the pony tail holder.

Now we're going to place all the loops from the starting edge onto the pegs, just like you would do for a loom knit hat with a folded brim. Locate the slip knot from your starting edge, and place that first loop on the starting peg.

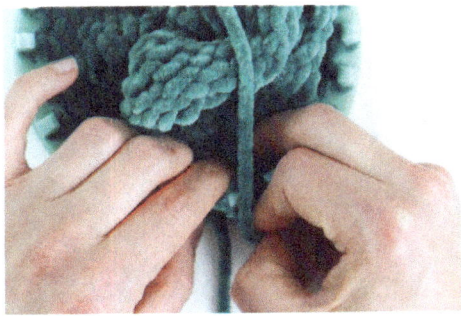

Then going around to the left, place each loop from the starting edge onto each peg.

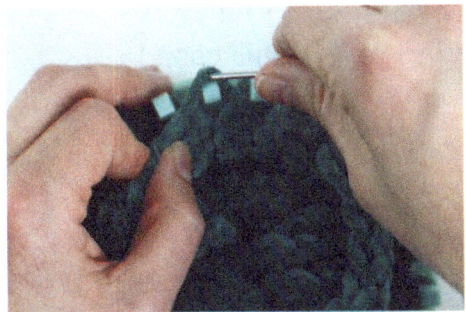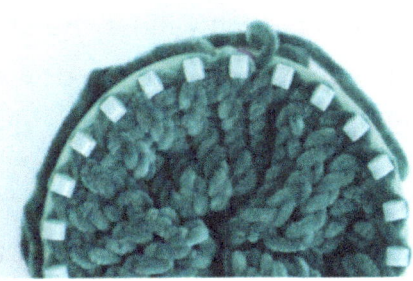

Once you get all the loops put on the pegs, knit the bottom loop up over the top loop and off the peg.

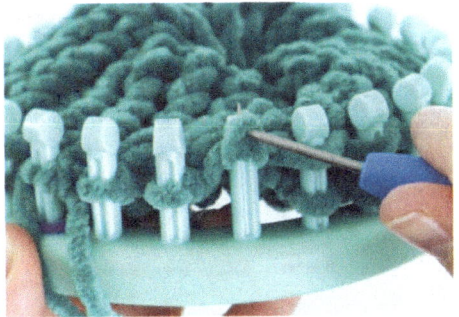

Repeat that around.

Step 4: Stretchy bind off

Pick up your yarn needle with the yarn tail threaded on it and now we're going to do our stretchy bind off.

Start by bringing the yarn down through the starting peg loop.

 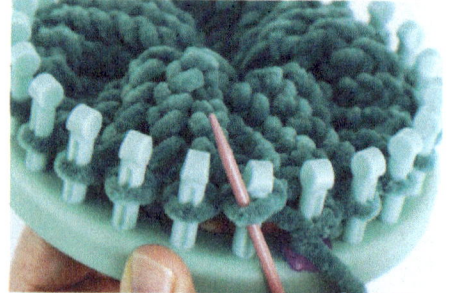

Then you're going to bring the needle up through the peg to the left.

Gently pull the yarn to tighten and bring it behind the peg to the right (which will be the starting peg in this case.)

Now you're going to go down through the loop to the right, and up through the peg to the left.

Step 5: Finishing up

Use the yarn needle to bring the long yarn end through the scrunchie so it's coming out at the same spot as the other yarn tail.

Infinity Scarf

3 -Way Wear * Infinity Scarf

Let me tell you a little about my scarf design. The Kalina Scarf is a two-toned, three-way wear, infinity wrap scarf. It can be worn as a long scarf, a double wrapped cowl, or a hood. It's worked on a 36-peg long loom, with a twisted stockinette st using a figure 8 wrap. The double knit creates a luxurious thick knitted fabric, twisted and stitched together at the ends. Pairing a hue with a neutral adds visual interest and gives the hue a bit of a boost!

Finished Measurements: 10"/25.4 cm w x 40"/1.02 m

Gauge: 7 sts and 10 rows = 4 inches in twisted stockinette stitch.

Level: Beginner

Yarn: Red Heart Soft, 100 % Acrylic, worsted #4 weight, 256 yd / (234m), 5oz / (141g), approx. 400 yds/365.8 m needed for the entire project.

- 1 skein, Color: Minty - #E728 4620
- 1 skein, Color: Off White - #E728 4601

Pattern Key

- ewk = e-wrap knit
- CO = cast on
- BO = bind off
- St (s) = stitch(es)
- A glossary of terms

Supplies

- Loom: ¾"/7.62 cm peg spacing, large gauge, 36 peg rake/rectangular/long loom
- Yarn/tapestry needle
- Knitting tool/loom hook
- Stitch markers (optional)
- Scissors
- Measuring tape

Pattern Notes

- This is a quick & easy loom knitting project, that produces an elegant looking scarf. Perfect for the beginner loom knitter.
- The scarf is made by knitting a long rectangle that is twisted once, and sewn together along the short edge.
- Two colors, held together as one, are used throughout pattern.
- Note: This is a double knit scarf and uses both sides of the loom.

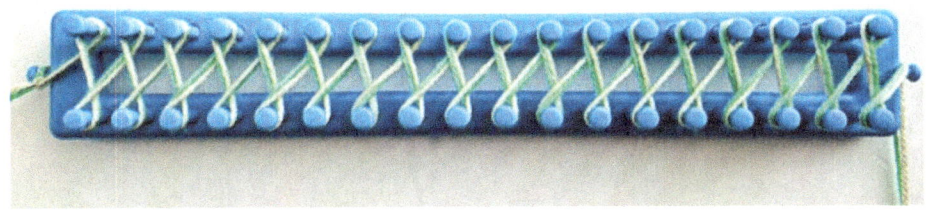

Infinity Scarf Pattern

Foundation Row: Using 2 strands, e-wrap CO the entire length of the loom, using the figure 8 wrap (see fig.1).
Row 1: Ewk all pegs, continuing to use the figure 8 wrap. Repeat row 1 until the body of the scarf is about 40 inches/1.02 m long or you are near the end of both skeins. Make sure you leave enough yarn to bind off the loom. Bind off, any method you prefer.

Finishing: Twist the scarf once, fold in half, and line up the cast on and the bind off edges (short ends) together to form a loop. Optional: Use your stitch markers to hold the two ends together evenly to make seaming easier. Using your yarn needle, sew the cast on edge to the bind off edge. Weave in ends.

Thanks
for
Reading

Made in United States
North Haven, CT
31 January 2025

65162339R00049